Angel Trippin'

CH Jodi M Dehn

Published by Tamerlane Media, 2024.

While every precaution has been taken in the preparation of this book, the publisher assumes no responsibility for errors or omissions, or for damages resulting from the use of the information contained herein.

ANGEL TRIPPIN'

First edition. January 1, 2024.

Copyright © 2024 CH Jodi M Dehn.

ISBN: 978-0983885382

Written by CH Jodi M Dehn.

Table of Contents

Introduction 1

CHAPTER 1 3

CHAPTER 2 6

CHAPTER 3 8

CHAPTER 4 10

CHAPTER 5 12

CHAPTER 6 15

CHAPTER 7 18

CHAPTER 8 20

CHAPTER 9 22

CHAPTER 10 24

CHAPTER 11 27

CHAPTER 12 30

CHAPTER 13 35

CHAPTER 14 64

CHAPTER 15 75

Acknowledgments

My Angels, first and foremost.

My protectors.

My light and love.

Then my Earth Angels who continue to support, inspire and motivate me. You know who you are.

And finally, my husband, Jeff. He supports, encourages, advises, loves me, and makes me laugh every day. My life travel buddy.

I love you all!

Introduction

"The world holds my adventure playground, traveling with my husband to multiple locations every year."

As an angel lightworker and intuitive empath, I've learned to trust my angel messages even when traveling - maybe more so when traveling. When checking out new adventures, I always ensure they know my itinerary well in advance to get maximum pop from my experiences.

I've found that it often depends on where I am that decides how the angels make me aware of their presence. It can vary from country to country. It can also vary depending on the energy of the location within a country.

It's been my experience that any archangel can and will present itself depending on the situation. Raphael will naturally be there because Raphael is the Archangel of travelers. Raphael always goes along for the ride.

Gabriel could present himself since he is all about joy-filled experiences. When you're traveling, that's what you're looking for—those moments and experiences that bring you joy.

CH JODI M DEHN

Michael could be on hand since he is the protector if a situation warrants protection. He's also the communicator of protection messages which is important if you're traveling internationally. Having Michael present to help you with any communication breakdowns eases any stress.

Patient Hanniel helps to relieve frustration and disappointment, giving you balance when those "totter" moments appear. Haniel lines up everything harmoniously. We all know that traveling has its pitfalls at times. That's where Haniel would step in.

I could go on about the different archangels, but I have so much to talk about.

Angels also may appear differently to different people in the same place, although they generally prefer certain energies. It's a matter of being present in the moment and understanding your gifts. If you've experienced supernatural/paranormal moments, you should be well on your way to discerning your angel trippin' messages.

My angels keep their bags packed, ready at a moment's notice for my adventures. I suggest activating your angels now to familiarize yourself with their different messaging energies. To learn more, go to Chaplain Jodi - Survivor Angels on Teachable.

Then once you're prepped, you'll be angel trippin' before you know it.

CHAPTER 1

Preppin' With the Angels

Here we go.

Before you leave on any adventure, you can do many things to ensure your angels are equally prepared. They always have their bags packed, but it helps if you can give them extra information—where you're going, what you'll be doing, who you'll be with. Anything pertinent to your trip.

Let's start with where you're going. Angels know everything, so for you to say, I'm going to Italy, I'm going to California, I'm going to Eastern Asia, that's fine. If you can give them more detailed information, that's better.

Talk to them about the specific places you're going. Talk about the cities, and the towns, and the villages. Then talk to them about the locations you'll be touring, staying, and possibly eating at. They take their cue from you as to how you talk about those places.

Angels are very busy energies, and doing this will help them focus on what you need. Their job is to bring you messages to ensure you have a wonderful trip.

The second piece involves what you'll be doing while you're there. Will you be traveling with family, friends, or strangers? Will you be walking a lot? Will you be involved in writing activities?

CH JODI M DEHN

Maybe you're going to be on a tour bus. You may be going places on segways, bicycles, canoes, or kayaks on waterways. You get the idea.

Next, clue your angels in on where you'll be staying. If you're going to be changing locations during your time away, they need to know that. That way, they can guide you on details you need to include in your pre-trip prep. It may be certain items that you need to bring. Clothing is a big piece unless you're going tropical. Then swimwear and a couple of pairs of shorts suffice. Preparing for any weather eventualities keeps you smiling on your travels.

Your angels can even help with places you may be eating. They may have great suggestions! They're probably already thinking about something on a particular menu that you should try. Then when you get to that restaurant, you'll be like, 'I think I'll have this' because the angels already planted that seed. It will be a wonderful epicurean moment for you.

As you're packing and prepping, continue talking to them.

As you're making your online arrangements, keep talking to them, and be open open open open open open open open open open. Just keep listening. They're going to guide you.

As you look at options and select different parts of your trip, the angels will continue to guide you. They know who you are; they know what you like. They'll find those little adventures that you've never tried before, too. Not to worry. They also know your limits.

ANGEL TRIPPIN'

Then, of course, if this is your first time traveling solo or it's the first time going to Italy or going across the Atlantic or the first time going to California, the first time on a plane, or on a train, and doesn't even have to be first times, still, it's something different from what you've done before. Again, the angels will help you make the best possible arrangements knowing you, what's available, and what challenges you may or may not be up for. The key is being present as you're doing all of this prep.

Activate those angels as you're doing your prep!

CHAPTER 2

Angel Trippin' Solo

I love to travel solo, but only for specific destinations. My husband and I make a great adventure team, but not everyone can say that.

For those of you who love solo travel or that's your only option - take heart. Your experiences can be amazing if you just adjust a few things.

Your angels are a must in solo status. They will consider things that you might not.

To best receive those messages, let's talk about your dreams. Angels love to bring you messages through dreams. They often come to you in your subconscious dreaming: meaning, when you wake up, you didn't even know that you dreamt.

As you prepare for your trip, keep a notepad and pen beside your bed. Get into this habit.

As soon as you wake up, close your eyes again. Check your third eye. Look deep into the darkness. If celestial messages came to you, subconscious or otherwise, your third eye brings them front and center.

ANGEL TRIPPIN'

It won't be the entire dream, but you'll see images, symbols, colors, or numbers. Write down whatever you see. Everything. If it doesn't make sense to you right now, it will. Process everything that you see each morning as a whole. The message or information that you need will be evident when the time is right.

When you're traveling, do the same thing. Angels will bring you information or ideas for the next day or a particular activity the same way.

Don't ignore these messages. You don't have someone else to bounce ideas off of as a solo traveler. You also don't have someone else to help you think of everything. But you do have your angels. Use them.

CHAPTER 3

Angel Trippin' with Friends

Trippin' with friends can be a joy or a curse, depending on how you plan. I've known friendships that have grown through travel. I've known friendships that have dissolved through travel.

Success lies in planning. Having everyone involved gives everyone a feeling of ownership and belonging. I'm a gatherer, so I'm a stickler on this.

If you've got a great organizer in your group, pull them in to take the lead. If you've got someone who's a great money cruncher, pull them in to help with budgets. If you've got someone who loves to plan parties and activities, pull them in to research those adventures.

Once you've done that, have a conversation with your angels. Point Jeremiel towards your organizer for clarity. Point Metatron toward your money cruncher for the best deals. Point Haniel toward your event planner for balance and harmony.

Then survey everyone else to see how they'd like to help.

While you're trippin', plan periodic check-ins. Zadkiel can help with the communication and discernment for the check-in. You want to make sure that everyone's experience is moving along positively.

You can hold these spontaneously or schedule. Your group personality will make this apparent.

ANGEL TRIPPIN'

Plan a 'memory' get-together once all the fun is over and you're home. The creativity that Gabriel lends will help to make this the perfect ending.

CHAPTER 4

Angel Trippin' with Family

Oh, the joys of family. Travel can test that to the max. Yikes!

If you involve everyone in the planning, though, young and old, you build accountability. Jophiel manifests goals and understanding for the fam as you plan.

Let everyone share their excitement and hopes for what they want to do. Make a note of all of them. Then get Jeremiel involved to help plan, making sure that you include something for everyone. You may have to get creative and combine some of the activities. As long as you've planned something from everyone's list, all should feel included.

Misunderstandings may still arise. When this happens, simply call in Raguel for guidance and Uriel to restore peace.

Another inclusive way to make sure everyone experiences their special request is to plan some things in smaller groups. Depending on how large your group is and the ages of the members, this helps the younger ones especially to feel included. Little ones can sometimes feel lost in a large group. Uriel loves to present new ideas.

The next thing you should set up for the whole family would be a primer on angels. Most of our grandkids understand how angels can make or break an event. They understand that angels bring positivity and light. They also understand that anything negative is off the table.

ANGEL TRIPPIN'

Traveling with family can be exhausting. There are so many personalities in motion. Sleep becomes a crucial part of the schedule. Don't overbook yourselves. Book sleep into your daily itinerary though. Samuel guides you in the sleep department.

Flexibility for family trippin' is a lifesaver. Keep your itinerary flexible. Some activities might not allow that, but when you can, flex that schedule as needed.

Reliving your adventure when you get home wraps it all up. The flubs, the excitement, the oopses, and the gifts, bring everyone full circle and back to center. Capture it all using everyone's inner child to find the gifts from every situation. If you need some help tapping your inner child just tap Chamuel.

CHAPTER 5

Flyin' with the Angels

On my way to Ft. Jackson, SC, for Army Chaplain Advanced School, we flew into a major storm outside of Atlanta. The sun had already set, so you could see the lightning streaking across the sky, illuminating angry clouds.

Our pilot was valiantly trying to keep that bird under control. Still, we were insanely pitching and rolling. If that wasn't bad enough, the storm forced many of the flights in the Atlanta area into a holding pattern, ours included. The sky was crowded.

More than half an hour passed, and still, there was no indication that we would be landing any time soon. Suddenly the plane began dropping and rising, the movement I hate the most, especially if I'm in the back of the plane—which I was.

It was angel time.

But before I could start, a flight attendant approached me.

"Are you a preacher?" she asked.

"Yes," I said.

I was surprised she even asked as I was traveling in uniform with the cross in full view on my lapel. In hindsight, I believe she was even more shook than I initially thought.

"Can we pray?" she asked.

ANGEL TRIPPIN'

"Oh, holy Hannah," I thought to myself. "We are in deep trouble."

She plopped down in the seat next to me and latched onto my hands in a death grip. I suggested that she fasten her seatbelt. She did.

Interestingly, I was never as terrified as she appeared to be. I believe it was because I knew angels were in control. They had our plane, the other planes still in the air, and those in the control tower. I know when they're in protective mode. Michael takes over, and you'll sense him in a warm, tingley way. I was tingley all over.

There wasn't a sound on that plane except for the faint sounds of others praying. You can't mistake the sound of whispered prayers.

The flight attendant and I prayed together. We prayed for probably 20 minutes until the pilot came on and announced that we were to prepare for landing. The collective exhale on that plane was audible.

I'll never forget that flight. It was so evident that those winged energies guided and directed everyone involved.

That was in the late 1990s, and ever since then, I've made it my responsibility to assess the flight attendants. The angels give me their nods to those who might be less sure or less experienced. Sometimes that information gets communicated to me through ringing in my ears. Other times it's repeated words or phrases in the initial boarding greeting. Still, other times I see a reflection of an angel aura near those who may need some support.

Other angel occurrences I've experienced while flying include angels directing people where to stow their carry-ons. I don't know if people realize it, but those who are in tune with their angels, knowingly or not, glide onto the plane, stow their bags, and get seated in one smooth movement. It's almost choreographed. Others clearly are clueless about their angel guides.

And then there are those who 'know.' Occasionally, another passenger sitting across the aisle or walking towards the bathrooms locks eyes with me, and a 'knowing' look is exchanged. That's probably Gabriel helping us to communicate our shared angel energy recognition.

Metatron jumps into flying mode, too. When there are children onboard, you can rest assured that Metatron claims a seat, too. He will help parents calm, entertain, and enjoy their children in flight. If you're a flying parent and can't seem to get a situation under control, just call on Metatron in light and love. He'll give you some excellent in-flight tools to get you through your pint-sized turbulence.

So, next time you fly, pay a little closer attention to some of these things and see if your angels don't pull you into their presence. There's nothing like flying with the angels.

CHAPTER 6

Surviving TSA and Customs

No one claims to be a fan of security checkpoints or custom stations. Travelers report feelings of anxiety, fear, impatience, and intolerance.

Have no fear. Your angels are always near. You just need to get them activated.

Example: My husband and I were in St. Petersburg, Russia, as part of a shore excursion on a Baltic cruise. We motored into St. Petersburg from our ship for two days, touring many amazing sights. On the second day, the motorcoach dropped us off at the customs station for reboarding our ship; we experienced a different turn of events from the first day.

Our tour guides instructed us not to engage in conversation with the customs agents and to maintain a serious demeanor.

My husband breezed through just as he did the first day. Not so much for me.

The female agent took my passport and ship paperwork and reviewed it. Then she started typing into her computer. Interesting point: the evening prior, at dinner, one of our table partners mentioned that she was worried about Russian customs as she was retired military. When my customs agent started typing into her computer, this conversation instantly popped into my head as I'm also a military veteran.

CH JODI M DEHN

My "safe" husband was standing a short distance away with a wondering look. All I could do was give him an 'I don't know' shoulder shrug.

As I turned to look back at the agent, she was handing my passport and paperwork to a male agent in the booth with her. Uriel is bathing me in peace now, and Zachariel is dousing me with strength - mental strength. Just as the female agent had done, the male agent was looking at my paperwork, looking at me, looking at the computer over and over and over and over.

Just as I was about to inquire about the delay, the male agent handed me my paperwork. I must have had a look on my face because the female agent said to me, "You look too young for your age." We all started to laugh, and I hastily said, "thank you" and joined my husband.

Another time, we were returning from Spain and the Mediterranean. We landed in New York before catching our connecting flight home. Due to mechanical issues, we were delayed leaving Barcelona. That put us scrambling in New York. I needed to get home as I was officiating a wedding the next day.

As we turned the corner in the airport to get into the customs line, all I could see was black. I had never seen so many Hasidic Jews. They were returning from a traditional trip to the Holy Lands. It was quite exhilarating for me.

And it was like hitting a brick wall. There was no way we would make our connecting flight.

Time to call in Jophiel. The game plan called for patience.

ANGEL TRIPPIN'

Finally, we reached the ticket counter to arrange another flight home. The agent wasn't having it. The soonest we could get out of NYC would be well after the wedding started. Time for some angel guidance. Gabriel obliged.

In clear, concise words, I informed the agent of my situation and the plight of a couple about to start their life together. He looked at me. He looked at my husband, who nodded affirmatively.

The agent said, "I can get you on the six a.m. flight. You'll arrive four hours before the wedding starts."

And with that, we received a voucher for a free hotel room, and taxi to and from the airport. And off we went.

Trust in your angels. They can work miracles in and through you.

CHAPTER 7

Cruisin' with the Angels

We love to cruise. It's a great way to see many places in a short amount of time on a budget.

Our angels have guided us every step of the way. They're particularly helpful in the pre-planning fun. Everything from selecting shore excursions to safety needs and local customs.

Most cruises stop in multiple countries, especially if you're on a longer one. That's where the angels can guide you with the local customs (I never want to be the 'rude American'.). The angels have helped us find some very informative television shows and online info that answer the questions to avoid offending anyone.

When we sailed the western Caribbean, one of our shore excursions involved kayaking in glass-bottom crafts. What a great experience. We never ventured out far, and they led us to some amazing underwater sites. When we finished and returned to shore, I wanted to tip the young boy who had done most of the hauling of the kayaks for us. He refused the tip. He said, "Not necessary. Your smile is all that I need." I'd forgotten that this was not an appropriate gesture. Angels kept me from offending one of the adults through the angelic response of this young man. Whew.

My husband wanted to explore some of the Mayan ruins in the Western Caribbean. This is when watching TV and online travel shows proved helpful once again. We knew which ones we'd get

ANGEL TRIPPIN'

to see, so we paid close attention to those sites featured on the shows. As we moved around the various locations, our research proved invaluable. There's not a lot of signage to preserve the sites' realistic state. Having that information ahead of time really gave us a step up. Thanks to Angel guidance, our research resources were appropriate for our destinations.

Italy has so much to see and do that cruising makes for the perfect first-time trip. You get a little taste of everywhere. While we haven't been back yet, we now know where we want to spend more time the next time we go.

One stop on this cruise was Pompeii, one of the most fascinating places in the world. Time stopped there when that volcano launched its fury. While we were part of a group with an amazing guide for most of this excursion, my husband and I still found little nuances that the Angels directed us to as we roamed the ruins in our free time. One area, a brothel, depicted some interesting scenes. Quite a surprise.

In comparing notes with other travelers, we received confirmation of the Angels' guidance for us. We were very fortunate to have discovered some of the things that we did.

CHAPTER 8

Ridin' the Rails with Angels

I love riding trains. I was six years old when I first rode a train. My family planned to travel from Bismarck, ND, to Portland, OR, to visit family for the holidays. My dad gave me his sense of adventure; at this young age, train travel was the ultimate thrill.

Back then, rail cars were coaches dating back to the 1940Ss. Vintage, to say the least. We traveled in the general seating car. I don't know if they had sleeper cars then, or maybe they were cost-prohibitive.

Traveling with so many other people just amped up my adventurous spirit. An avid reader, I regaled those around us reading riddles. Even the conductors would stop and join in. It was, after all, a two-day trip, and Gabriel wanted to keep everyone happy.

As we traveled through the days and nights with a wintry landscape as our view, I found myself mesmerized by the beauty of it all. It encompassed sights, sounds, smells, and feelings I'd never experienced before. Archangel Ariel must have purchased a ticket, too.

The second time I was fortunate enough to travel by train, the Vista Dome cars were in vogue. Now looking out over that same landscape, although this time in the Summer, sitting high atop a rail car, provided a whole new adventure.

ANGEL TRIPPIN'

Since those early adventures, I've traveled several other times by train. As an adult, I was more cognizant of my angels. They constantly pointed out more sights, sounds, smells, and feelings that I'd either forgotten or hadn't noticed when I was younger. Thanks, Ariel.

The angels also prompted me to try new things. I exited the train at several stops and explored the train stations even though traveling solo. Each stop was different from the rest. I also ate in the dining car several times. I'd done that with my parents, but it was a different experience being on my own as I was seated with strangers. I felt at ease with Michael providing protection, Uriel amping my discernment, and Raphael handling everything else. Thanks to their presence and support, I felt quite at ease, although alert to anything concerning.

Subway and metro trains pose a slightly different undertaking. Your travel distance is shorter, so you've got to think faster. Also, there are slight differences between the UK trains and American subways. It pays to check these out ahead of time.

Depending on the city, most subways in the U.S. can be an economical and reasonably safe means of transportation. We rode Boston's subway from the suburbs into the heart of Boston and back out. I found angel messages in the signage inside the cars and the billboards we sped past.

In the UK, namely London, we successfully navigated the city thanks to Jeremiel, who provided clarity whenever we debated a destination stop. Jeremiel always steered us right.

CHAPTER 9

Motorcoachin' with the Angels

I've traveled a bit on buses—more tour buses than commercial ones. I don't really have a preference. It all depends on my adventure. I have, however, had angel experiences on both.

My first one happened when I was 18. My grandmother had passed. I was away at college and, coincidentally, touring with my university band. I left the tour in Minneapolis to travel to North Dakota, where the funeral would take place.

It was winter, just after the holidays. Good old Greyhound Bus Lines carried people on our highways. I don't remember how I got to the Minneapolis bus station. Still, I remember sitting there waiting for the bus that would take me up through Fargo and on to my destination.

I was young but looked younger than my age. For anyone else, the red flags would've been flying like crazy. The downtown Minneapolis bus station, even back in the 1970s, was no place for someone my age. Let alone being alone for very long. But I remained quite at ease.

I traveled lightly since the band tour lasted only a few days. In this case, that was good as I didn't have to stow my one small suitcase under the bus. I could keep it with me.

ANGEL TRIPPIN'

The bus driver was a very kind gentleman helping me on and off the bus at some of our many stops. Now, I was young and competent so...hmmm...why was helping me? Only when I reached my destination, and he assisted me again did I realize why he'd been so kind.

He thought that I was pregnant.

Back then, part of the fashion was empire-style tops, much like maternity tops—my attire for this trip. I chalk it up to the angels giving me some added protection through an earth angel while trippin' solo.

When it comes to tour buses, the same holds true. Earth Angels come to us through people from all walks of life. I find it fascinating that sometimes when I travel, if I'm perplexed, confused, or completely lost on something, the fog clears thanks to someone I'm 'casually' traveling with.

For example, I met many Earth Angels on our tour bus trip through Ireland. Several psychics provided a great deal of information on ancestors at the medieval sites we visited. There was the energy worker who cleared up some of the angel energy confusion that I was experiencing in this super-charged angelic country. I also found a Celtic Angel right on the bus, checking off one of my missions while in Ireland.

I highly recommend traveling by bus for the Earth Angel connections. They add so much to your adventure.

CHAPTER 10

Road Trippin' with the Angels

I've loved road trips since I was a kid. Every summer, my family hopped in our station wagon and set out for new destinations, usually West. I'm so thankful that they believed travel provided educational opportunities. It's an education that can't be matched any other way.

Given our large family and great circle of friends, we could spend several days and nights with them as we arrived at new locales. The angels were always prompting me with questions to ask to learn more about them, where they lived, and things that were special to the area we were visiting. Locals, after all, provide the best source of information for non-tourist hotspots.

Angels also yelled out protective messages when we were attempting new activities.

The first time visiting Yellowstone I clearly was not grasping the danger of the geysers. I'd run along the boardwalks and jump on the rails without a second thought. Earth Angels were sent to bring the threat into focus in my young brain. I received several very stern warnings from strangers, obviously knowing my impetuous mind.

Another time we were at the Reptile Gardens in South Dakota. I ran full tilt and hopped up on the crocodile tank railing. The roar that came back at me from about a half dozen people was definitely an angelic 'choir' in full voice.

ANGEL TRIPPIN'

As we traveled our nation's highways, the angels again pointed out sights I might not have seen. They also whispered insights to me that could only have come from them. I would not have been capable of those thoughts at a young age, even though I am an intuitive empath.

As an adult, road trips remain one of my favorite ways to travel.

One year my husband and I flew into London, rented a car, and took off for adventures unknown. Our first reckoning came when we realized London is a complicated city to drive in. Plus, the GPS in our rental car was programmed in German, so we were flying by the seat of our pants. Thankfully, Gabriel giddily whispered to me that I could semi-translate the street names, having taken three years of German in high school.

Leaving London, we headed for Bath, England. We drove rather aimlessly in Bath, looking for a particular historic site. Deciding to take a shortcut down a lesser traveled street, we suddenly heard a loud sound. Stopping, we got out and discovered that our left front tire was blown. Moving towards the trunk, I found we'd also blown the left rear tire. Dang. We only had one spare.

Not knowing what the best course of action was, we called the rental car company. They instructed us to call the car company. The car company informed us that we'd have to replace the tires at our expense as it wasn't a maintenance issue. They would call an on-the-road service vehicle to come and help us at no charge. Angel gift number one.

CH JODI M DEHN

Surprisingly, we only waited about a half hour for the service vehicle. In a matter of minutes, the driver had one tire replaced with our spare and the other with a spare that he carried. He then instructed us to follow him to a nearby service garage, where they would have us on our way in no time.

Truer words were never spoken. The garage was only about three blocks away, and the staff knew we needed to get back on the road as expeditiously as possible. In another 30 minutes, that's precisely where we were—back on the road. Earth Angels came to us in superhero fashion.

On another trip crossing from Nevada into Utah, we realized that gas might become a concern. We were dropping fast. Then we started seeing billboards for The Oasis service station. Yea! We were close. Sure, we were close, but there were no pumps or people when we arrived. There was nothing there. Nothing.

Back on the road we went. We were so low on gas that neither my husband nor I said a word. We were collectively holding our breath, willing that vehicle to keep going. Raphael came through and got us to a gas station with the car still running. The amount of gas that my husband pumped into the vehicle was as much as the tank held. We were truly driving in on a wing, an angel wing, and a prayer.

Never stop believing. Just remember to act on what the angels tell you.

CHAPTER 11

Bikin' with the Angels

Rolling down the highway on a motorcycle gives you all kinds of opportunities to know that your angels are present.

One time we were traveling on our bikes with our daughter and her husband, heading for a paranormal event, and we knew bad weather was coming. Since I was riding as a passenger, I pulled up the radar on my cell phone. It was still a ways off, so we kept riding. And I kept checking.

I looked up into the sky, and there as prominent as ever hovered an angel in the clouds. I pointed it out to everybody, and they all remarked that we really needed to start watching the weather. That angel cloud stayed in the same position for a half hour. In that half hour, storm clouds rolled in. It was interesting because that angel cloud started to fade, but I could still discern it from the rest of the clouds.

The radar changed, and we knew we needed to get off the road. As soon as we realized that, the angel cloud disappeared.

It just so happened that about two miles from where we called it, there was a cute little out of the way, out in the country, bar and restaurant that we could conveniently pull into to wait out the storm. Our timing wasn't perfect, and we got a bit wet, but thanks to Raphael giving us that message up in the clouds, we escaped a drenching.

CH JODI M DEHN

Riding a motorcycle is one of the most exhilarating ways to travel. It's also one of the most dangerous ways to travel. So before we head out, I always call in the angels. In addition to Raphael, our traveling angel, I also call in Michael, because he is the protector. Depending on where we're going, I will call in other angels I think might be necessary, with the final little tagline of "If anyone else would like to join us, please do."

I always thank my angels.

I will talk to them as we're riding. I keep checking in with them. I don't pray to them. I don't consider angels to be God or gods. I simply talk to them like I would talk to my husband, my kids, or a good friend, and I always speak to them respectfully.

I never get upset with them, even though I might be upset. It's not on them because they will only bring messages of light and love and positivity and protection. If I'm not smart enough to listen, it's on me.

When we're out on our bikes, the angels are our eyes, our ears, our everything. They take care of us. They bring us messages—even ones that we don't expect.

Another time we'd set out on a four-day trip with friends on a Monday morning in June. There were scattered rain showers. I don't know any bikers that like riding in the rain. To avoid the big dumps, we changed our route and missed most of it.

With the reroute, we stopped at a bar/restaurant near one of our good friends. My husband called him to join us for lunch.

His phone was disconnected.

ANGEL TRIPPIN'

My husband Googled him.

His obituary came up.

We found out from the restaurant staff that his passing was unexpected. Quite the kick in the gut for us. What we realized, though, was that the angels rerouted us so we'd end up there and find this out.

As we finished lunch and got back on the road, my right ear started ringing. That always means angels are bringing in a message. I closed my eyes, and in my third eye I saw our deceased friend coming up next to us on his bike. He had his usual mischievous grin, and it was as if he was telling us that he was doing just fine.

We stopped for gas a bit later. I was telling our friends and my husband about this when my husband said, "I saw the same thing at about the same time." Thank you, angels!

I love riding. Rolling thunder with angels has a whole new meaning. But remember, your angels are warriors for you to ride hard, ride on, and ride safely.

CHAPTER 12

Sleepin' with the Angels

Hotels

When it comes to hotels, they are about as diverse as it gets for angels. If you think about it, the people who have passed through those doors and slept in those beds vary greatly. It only makes sense that the angels that present themselves will be equally diverse.

How they present themselves to you at hotels will also vary. You could hear repetitive phrases. It could be repetitive lyrics or even a single song lyric. At that point, it gives you the answer to something you're contemplating.

You can also see the angels, especially in hotels. They present themselves by repeated colors or a flash of light in their aura color or with the appearance of a dime or penny or repetitive numbers.

You could also get a little chill all of a sudden. I call it a willy—that's what my grandpa always used to call it. There are also the light sparkles or the sweeps of color that appear in your peripheral vision. There are any number of ways that Angels present themselves.

Oh...Don't forget about the orbs. People like to poo-poo the orbs. A certain percentage of people believe that orbs are nothing more than dust, dirt, or moisture in the air. You can tell if it's an angel orb, though, when you enlarge the photo; you'll

ANGEL TRIPPIN'

see a shape in it. Generally, the shape will be that of a halo, but it's not limited to that. While in Ireland, at a gaol/ jail, a group member captured an orb in a photo with a halo in the middle of it. The halo couldn't be clearer.

When it comes to hotels, be wide open. Just open yourself up because all the angels are there. They never leave you. When you need them, just call them in. Craft your intention in light and love, even if it's just to get a good night's sleep. You're exhausted from the day, but you're all wound up? Call on Samuel in light and love. Talk to them with your positive intention. Thank them and say good night for a peaceful slumber.

This is even more important if you're staying at a haunted establishment.

My husband and I were road trippin' back from the west coast. We decided to spend the night at a haunted hotel in Wyoming. Remember, you get what you ask for. We asked for a haunted room.

In the middle of the night, my husband woke from a dead sleep and jumped out of bed, looking like he'd seen a ghost. That's close. A little girl had whispered in his ear. Not a dream. A for-real whisper. I've never seen him move so fast.

Pleasant dreams...angel dreams.

B & Bs

We've had some great adventures headquartered out of B&Bs. We've also had a few that had the angels moving quickly and moving us quickly.

CH JODI M DEHN

We took a bike trip to Nashville with three friends. The ride was great except for hitting Nashville traffic on a Summer Sunday afternoon with everyone returning from their weekend getaways.

Angels did get us safely to our B&B. The B&B impressed all of us. New. Contemporary. Spacious. Comfortable. Very nice.

After unpacking the bikes, we needed some provisions for our three-day stay. Checking Google, we found a convenience store about six blocks away.

Having spent enough time on our bikes, we decided to walk. Six blocks is doable.

As we came around the first corner, we started questioning the area that we were in. It didn't match the previous block where we were staying.

Continuing, we soon realized that this was not the part of town to be walking through. There was a drug deal going down on one corner. People were doing drugs in the front yard of a home. Ruh Roh.

Angel alert. Time to move a little faster. Everyone appeared friendly, or maybe it was because we were all dressed like bikers that they were wary of us rather than the other way around. We acknowledged them but didn't engage. Archangel Michael had us almost double timing by the end of that first questionable block.

ANGEL TRIPPIN'

Reaching the convenience store, we found the front encased in metal bars with large locks on the door. Going inside, we quickly learned that this was a possible front for some illegal transactions and not a stop for milk and eggs.

While exiting, two of us already had our cell phones out, searching for another convenient store. Two others noticed several squad cars driving down the street.

The next closest store was several miles away, so it was Uber time. ETA six minutes. It took about 15 minutes and felt like 60 for it to arrive.

Thanks to our quick thinking, and Archangel Michael's help, we managed to avoid a bad situation. Lesson: let your angels guide you when selecting your B&B to ensure that the neighborhood matches the quality of the rental.

Camping

Camping remains high on our list of travel accommodations. Our entire family is well-versed in this fun summer adventure.

When my husband and I first met, we headed north for a somewhat rustic camping experience. We stayed at a state park, but the tent sites were slightly more out of the way than the camper sites.

The first night a storm came up. We did everything we could do to keep the tent from lifting off. The campground sat high on a bluff overlooking Lake Superior and the lightening show was spectacular.

CH JODI M DEHN

As we lay there trying to sleep, the wind literally swirling around us, I heard Archangel Gabriel. If you don't know, Gabriel can be a real Chatty Kathy. On this night, he simply said, "Sleep." With that, I knew that all was well or indeed would be.

Camping with the family brings on a different perspective. You need to plan for kid, adult, and family activities. Here's where the tips I presented in Angel Trippin' with the family can be implemented.

Even then, things won't go exactly as planned, so just let the angels lead. In other words, relax and enjoy.

CHAPTER 13

Destinations

Great Britain

Crossing the pond to explore England, Wales, and Scotland, I found angels popping up everywhere. They love to guide you both audibly (clairaudience) and visually (physical sight & clairvoyance) here. You'll see and hear their messages in repetitive signage, village music, conversations, and as part of historical trappings. Often I found myself wanting to become part of the moment or place thanks to the angel leadings.

England

Traveling by car in Great Britain is truly a one-of-a-kind experience. It doesn't matter what British country you're exploring, they all drive on the left side of the road. If you're American or from another country that drives on the right side of the road, it is a challenge.

We made one trip to England, Wales, and Scotland, driving it in about ten days. We drove 1,500 miles. It was insane.

I already regaled you with the story of our blown tires and the earth angels that came to our rescue. It indeed was amazing. We still talk about it. The courtesy, the helpfulness, and the kindness could only come from angels...earth angels.

Wales

We continued to Wales and hit rush hour when we entered Cardiff. We were so lost.

The only thing to do was to call the hotel and hope they could help us. A wonderful young woman answered. She said, "You're not the first person this has happened to. I would be happy to guide you." That's what she did. She directed us beautifully through heavy traffic and unknown streets.

We arrived at the hotel safe and sound. We headed inside, got to the counter, and I explained who I was. I knew the woman's name who'd helped us on the phone, so I asked for her. She was standing off to the side.

I said, "I need to give you a hug because after the day that we've had, you literally are an angel."

I gave her a huge hug and she said, "Wow! I've never been called an angel before."

"You are an Earth Angel," I said. "Our Earth Angel. Your whole attitude brought total calm and peace to us after a very crazy day." She truly carries Haniel with her.

Scotland

Ah, Scotland. I must have spent a previous life there. It called to me. It calls to me now.

Our only visit to date was a whirlwind road trip. You might describe it as a drive-by. We were so taken with it, though, we plan to go back and live there for a month sometime soon.

ANGEL TRIPPIN'

Sandalphon, the Archangel of music, locks up Scotland. Everywhere I looked, everything I touched, and everything I encountered held its own melody. Scotland, for me, played like a symphony.

The synchronicity was astonishing. The history and culture played out as a musical masterpiece.

We toured the underground tunnels of Edinburgh after wandering the castle for several hours. In those tunnels, Sandalphon brought out a chorus of voices from the past that sang every emotion of those souls.

After a full day exploring Edinburgh on foot, we rested in a tiny restaurant crammed with patrons. As we ate our meal, listening to the conversations around us, it felt like we'd been woven into their lives.

Thank you, angels. 'Til we meet again in Scotland.

Ireland

And then there's Ireland.

Angels in Ireland are industrious energies. For me, they were constantly talking to me. I'd see them as colors, sparkles, and 'mists' in my peripheral vision and boldly in front of me. Another traveler with our group confirmed many of those experiences, and sharing those encounters was really fun.

CH JODI M DEHN

At the Hellfire Club just outside of Dublin, negative forces pushed and pushed to keep me out of the ruin. I was very apprehensive about entering anyway. After calling in my angels and several attempts to push in, the dark energy I'd encountered moved, and I could enter. Michael communicated that nicely.

First, I explored the ground floor. Then I moved to the second. As I was about to leave one room, I looked up. Cobalt blue sparkles hovered above me. Not dust. Not dirt. No moisture in the air. I could remove those things from the angel energy hovering above me. Michael came. Michael communicated his protective presence to me just as I had requested before entering the Hellfire Club.

And then there's the elemental who attempted to 'hug' me, and a murdered priest doing the play-by-play. Knowing that your angels have you covered means everything.

We were investigating Leap Castle near Offaly, Ireland—probably the most haunted castle in the world. My husband and I visited there 22 years earlier on our honeymoon doing a leisurely afternoon tour with the owner, Sean Ryan. This time we were with Mysterious Adventures Tours.

On this night, the setting was straight out of a Hollywood movie. Cold. Rainy. And a wind that tested the sturdiest of trees. You could almost hear the banshees screaming through it.

ANGEL TRIPPIN'

We'd moved up to the Bloody Chapel with a local paranormal team, Paranormal Adventures Ireland, which investigates Leap regularly. As they directed us to form a circle, the wind suddenly picked up. Windows were non-existent on that top floor, so the energy sensation from this wind was palpable.

As we began our work, one para team member, a channeler, instructed the "woman in the white scarf" to step into the middle of the circle. That woman was me.

In a matter of minutes I began to sway, encircled by the rest of my group. The channeler almost immediately started communicating a message to me that he was receiving. "You will be okay," he said over and over. The more I swayed, the more muted my hearing became. It's something my angels do to protect me. I felt as though I had moved into a trance-like state. Based on a previous, similar experience, the para team moved me out of the circle for my safety.

The wind grew fiercer as I sat on a stone ledge. With the eerie lights from the investigation, the sound of the wind, and the shadows cast on the walls, it was surreal for everyone. The 'feeling' that enveloped me that started with the swaying stayed with me until we left the castle, even though attempts were made to clear me, even one attempt directed by me.

Comparing notes with the para team afterward, they affirmed that the message the channeler received came from the murdered priest. It was to reassure me that I would be okay against the attempts by the elemental to overtake me. The team also affirmed that there was no doubt that I was wrapped in angel protection the entire time I was within the walls of the castle. The angels had my back.

The Baltic

Traveling to the Baltic countries brings an entirely different angel vibe. Angels appeared more through feelings and emotions, at least for me being an empath.

In Estonia and Russia, I experienced heavier messages and some anxiety even though I loved Russia and look forward to returning someday. The opaque messages carried more serious thoughts, and there was some hesitation in the communication. I found that very interesting.

When clearing customs to leave Russia, I was detained by two Russian customs agents. My husband had smoothly passed through ahead of me.

I began to get concerned when the first agent called over the second. I could feel angel wings wrapping around me, protecting me, as I stood silently. After what seemed like an eternity, I was allowed to pass through. Once I'd cleared the area, the "wrap" disappeared.

Sensations were the complete opposite in the Scandinavian countries and the Netherlands. The energy in those countries felt bright and uplifting. Celestial messages were coming through as less serious feelings. Angel "gut" guidance or clairsentience was pervasive, and that's always good angel guidance.

ANGEL TRIPPIN'

In Stockholm, we ventured out to the oldest town in the beautiful country of Sweden. After the formal tour, my husband and I went to a tiny restaurant to grab lunch. The building was the oldest in town and the menu featured authentic ethnic foods. Growing up with a Norwegian/Swedish grandmother, I knew a little about some of the dishes. Time to call in the angels for some discernment, though. They obliged. Our lunch proved to be a wonderful treat.

Arriving back in Stockholm, we toured a museum that housed a restored ship that sank in 1628, the Vasa. Talk about time trippin'. Not even Hollywood could capture the look and scope of that sailing marvel.

We couldn't board it, but there was a beautiful platform around it to get an up-close look. As we casually made our way around this impressive restoration, I sensed angel presence. The angel presence wasn't for us, though. It was for the spirits that remained attached to their vessel. This feeling was new to me. It allowed me to get an "out of body" type glimpse at those souls who'd attempted to sail this majestic ship so long ago.

As for Finland and Denmark, angel messages here gave me moments of great discernment as we toured and visited villages and sites. I found that moments, and connections to these countries, resonated more profoundly thanks to angel messages that sparked deeper reflection. Messages came through just about all of my claires, depending on location.

CH JODI M DEHN

In Denmark, our lunch took us on a culinary adventure. Our restaurant host described the origins of the ingredients and the recipes right down to why their ancestors felt they needed these foods. We were served each food individually rather than all at once. It reminded me of a finely choreographed performance. These earth angels gave us an unforgettable gift.

The Mediterranean

There's nothing like visiting France for the first time and seeing a wedding erupt into an all-out street brawl.

One of our first stops on our Mediterranean cruise was in Nice, France on the French Riviera. Stunning. We spent the day on a shore excursion trippin' the neighboring countryside. We visited a small, intimate village with cobblestone sidewalks, meandering through quaint shops. We ate lunch at an outdoor cafe and got our first taste of French wine.

We enjoyed lunch with a couple from Australia who've become great friends. Archangel Chamuel made an excellent match for a lifelong friendship.

After lunch, we were dropped off along the beaches of Nice to explore at our leisure. Walking the Riviera's version of a boardwalk, we suddenly noticed a commotion. We followed the sound and discovered a wedding party and guests moving quickly through the streets of Nice.

We asked a local, who was also watching, if they knew what was happening.

ANGEL TRIPPIN'

Apparently the bride found out the groom still had a girlfriend. She left him at the altar moments before the wedding. The bride's brothers were getting into the middle of it. Families and friends were all part of the crowd. Passionate yelling echoed everywhere. Bystanders like us grew in number. It was quite the sight.

They needed some angel intervention.

In Montenegro, our shore excursion took us deep into the countryside. The only roads in and out of the port were switchbacks, which lend themselves poorly to the big tour buses. We arrived late to our restaurant for dinner, which was incredibly delish.

This also meant that we were late returning to our ship. We walked through a street festival as we headed to the boat that would return us to the ship. It was magical. Angels highlighted smells, sounds, and sights for us. There was so much going on.

By now, it's dark. As our boat leaves the dock, we were entertained by the festival lights. Looking up, we were graced with a beautiful, starry night sky accompanying us back to the ship.

Appreciation for this beauty truly came through the angels.

The Caribbean

In Caribbean countries with ocean breezes, you'll find your angel messages coming through in the wind and smells floating on those winds.

Wind direction often tells you which archangel is communicating. North will be Uriel. South will be Michael. East means Raphael. West means Gabriel. Listen to the wind for the messages, and you will get a better idea of which angel is communicating and, based on their gifts and abilities, the message they're bringing you.

With smells, it will be those scents associated with the different archangels. For example, Zadkiel brings us the aromas of orange, lavender, or rosewood, whereas Metatron holds more spicy or herbal aromas. Not everyone will experience the smells, just like not everyone will tune in audibly to the angels.

Island countries like the Dominican Republic give you a snapshot of life juxtapositions. You have affluent, all-inclusive resorts with poverty surrounding them. It gives you pause, especially when the angels highlight these.

When we were leaving the Dominican Republic from Punta Cana the second time, our departure took a bumpy turn.

We finally were on the plane after surviving a remarkably long line at the airport to get through customs. We're sitting in line to take off. Finally, it's our turn. The pilot maneuvers the plane onto the runway and then makes an announcement: "Ladies and gentlemen, I am sorry to say that we must return to the terminal. We have a hydraulic fluid leak, and for us to take off would be a disaster."

Back to the terminal for us.

ANGEL TRIPPIN'

As we disembarked the plane after sitting on it for about an hour and a half, we looked underneath the plane. Crews had put a life raft there to catch the leaking hydraulic fluid. It was amazing the amount of fluid streaming out. The pilot would never have been able to land that plane. We don't even want to think about the end game.

Thankfully, the people from the radio station who were in charge of our tour started scrambling. They needed to find us a place to stay for the night. Where we had been staying, at one of the all-inclusives, didn't have room for us anymore.

Our lead tour guides needed to find us something else. They also needed to find another bus to transport us, because the airline said it would be at least a day before they could secure another plane to take us home.

All the arrangements took about four hours. Finally we were heading out of the airport. We were on the bus for a good half-hour. We'd been told we were heading for a four-star resort and would only be there one night.

We arrive at our overnight accommodation and realize it's Spring Break. Plus, we arrived at a time of the night when the Spring Breakers were beyond coherent. We'd just been dropped at party central. We all checked into our rooms and said good night; we were all dead tired. That night, though, seemed longer than most. We couldn't wait to get back on the bus and head for the airport.

CH JODI M DEHN

The next morning at the airport terminal we needed to go through customs all over again, even though we'd done it the day before. Then the miracle happened. They started boarding us on the plane... a brand new beautiful plane.

My husband and I sat next to a young college student. She asked, "Were you two on the disaster flight?"

We laughed and said, "Yes, if that's what you want to call it."

"Well, let me reassure you," she said, "that you are in good hands on this one because it's my dad flying this plane." Angels, angels, angels everywhere.

Throughout the whole experience, I never saw red flags. I think because I knew the angels were in control. The angels told our first pilot "Don't go - don't take off. Check those dials. Check all of your readings." And the pilot got the message. I was so thankful for that, as well as the radio station that took such excellent care of us and managed to get everything to fall into place. I wouldn't say it was easy for them, but it wasn't excruciating, either. They were listening to angels, too.

Punta Cana, Dominican Republic, is a beautiful place. We ventured out on a few tours that took us off the all-inclusive resort and through poverty-stricken areas. We learned how people work to get their education and then move into starting higher-up jobs. The resorts play a big part in that.

Part of our trip involved bringing school supplies to local children. Each group member brought a backpack filled with basic school necessities. We were humbled to present those to the children, who were so excited and so grateful to receive such simple things. It was like they all became little angels that reflected back to us. Truly an incredible experience.

US of A

Hawaii

Ooh, Hawaii! Love those ocean breezes and the sand between your toes and the warm sun on your face. It's paradise.

On our first venture across the Pacific to the island of Oahu, we booked a B&B. Talk about a perfect way to start a trip in paradise.

We slept with the windows open. The rustling of banana trees outside our window lulled us to sleep. The food grounded us as we experienced feasts from the best of the island.

The first B&B was only available for a couple of nights. We'd reserved a room at another B&B for the remaining nights.

I should've listened closer to my angels. That B&B was on a different island, which meant another flight.

I called my angels, and they seamlessly got the reservation canceled without any fees. But now what?

We were there to visit our oldest child, who was stationed at Schofield Barracks. His family lived in one of the small apartments on the post.

CH JODI M DEHN

We called him and he suggested we stay on post at the hotel. Since I'm prior service military, we got the veteran rate, saving us some cha-ching. Crisis averted.

When you're in Hawaii, you'll find that your angels enjoy the sun, surf, and sand with you.

The best way to recognize angels' presence on these beautiful islands is through your clairalience, or sense of smell. All the angels carry certain scents, and I've put a guide in the glossary for you to reference.

I encourage you to challenge yourself while in Hawaii, or anywhere else, to see if you "smell" an angel near you at different times and locations. See if you can pick out your angels in between the fragrances and aromas that make Hawaii what it is.

Take a moment. Be present in the moment. Think about what you're doing, what you're seeing, what you're hearing, and possibly even what your expectations are. Then just sit back. You can find a lot of places to sit and relax and lounge. Close your eyes and inhale. Try to pull out a scent that sticks out. Something a little different.

It might be something that is native to Hawaii. You have to be very discerning if you need an angel message at that point. If you do not need one, then you're probably just inhaling part of the beauty of Hawaii. If you need a message though, whether it's just to get yourself grounded and balanced again or if you're contemplating if you're tired, need food, or need to just move on, then be aware. Your angel will help you make that determination.

ANGEL TRIPPIN'

When you go to the beautiful islands of Hawaii, know that your angels are with you. Their bags are always packed. They've got a swimsuit every time. I wonder if they wear Speedos or trunks.

The Southeast

The southeastern part of the U.S. is a collision of cultures against a backdrop of history. Dating back to pre-colonial times through the Civil War and the cultural upheaval of the 1960's, the Southeast holds angels around every corner.

We traveled to Key West with a radio tour group. Between 60 - 70 people made the trip. Getting there was an event in and of itself.

Leaving Minneapolis in a snowstorm is not for the faint of heart. Our group was split between several flights. Going through several de-icings only to sit and wait longer on the tarmac set us back for two future connections. This was one of those occasions where I called in all of the angels. So many processes were in motion to get us up and away that I thought we needed an "all call."

Of course, we eventually took off and got to our first connection. We were late. No surprise. The airline failed to make any arrangements for rescheduling 60-70 travelers. It was a nightmare.

I asked Jophiel to send clarity to the airline schedulers to get things moving. We were about halfway through the group when suddenly things began clicking.

About half of our group was able to get out quickly. Then there were others like us who had a two-hour wait.

We finally got on our next flight and to our next connection—but late, of course. This time, though, the airline was ready for us. Thank you, Jophiel.

We walked to the plane and realized it was one of those "little" planes. I call them puddle-jumpers. Gulp. I don't like those "little" planes. I needed some courage...a lot of courage. Michael to the rescue. Michael isn't called the "angel in charge" without good reason. Courage arrived.

A final note: we arrived in Key West after the airport closed. We had no idea how we would get our luggage or get to our hotel. Raphael came to the rescue again. Out of nowhere, a custodian appeared. He was as surprised to see us as we were to see him. He called someone. We got our luggage. Taxis appeared. On with our vacation.

While in Key West, eight of us decided one day that we wanted to go jet skiing on the ocean. Coming from Minnesota, everyone in our group had been snowmobiling before; the majority of our group had been jet skiing before, too, either on a lake or a river. My husband and I had not jet skied, but we had snowmobiled since we were kids. Let me say—snowmobiling is not the same as jet skiing and especially jet skiing on the ocean.

I am not a big water person. I don't like being around water; I like my feet firmly on the ground. So I was already calling in my angels before we ever started those machines and headed out.

ANGEL TRIPPIN'

One of the things that you have to do with a jet ski is know how to hit the waves to minimize the impact. Otherwise you get slammed. I have a chronic back condition, so this is crucial for me.

Sadly this didn't go as planned. Every time we hit a wave, it was like a lightning bolt searing through my back. My husband did his absolute best to minimize it, and I applaud him. I've had the back condition since 1975, so I've learned to manage it pretty well. Everybody else was having a great time. The last thing that I wanted was to spoil anybody's fun by saying I had to go back.

Our ride was about an hour out and an hour ride back. We stopped on a sandbar for a bit and slowed down in a couple of other places to check in with everybody.

One of the members of our group, who is quite advanced on a jet ski, was so caught up in the fun that he wound up somersaulting off his machine and into the air. Luckily, he wasn't hurt. He was just fine. He thought it was fun, so my take is that the angels protected him too. I'm glad that I called in the angels for everyone on that ride. Way to go, Michael.

Then there's Savannah, GA. A city haunted by its war-torn past. It's beautiful. It's welcoming. It's deceptively serene.

You can walk the length and breadth of the heart of Savannah easily. The parks are always alive with people passing through or just relaxing.

Where you get the true picture of Savannah, though, shows up down by the waterfront. It's the ultimate step back in time.

Sitting at a bar waiting for our table in one restaurant, I could feel angel presence. Nothing scary. I just knew the angels were hovering.

It was only a matter of minutes after discovering them that the bartender struck up a conversation with us.

"Do you believe in ghosts or spirits?" she asked.

My husband and I looked at each other and back at her. We basically said to her, "What have you got?"

She proceeded to tell us several stories about the restaurant and its history, filling our table wait time. Thank you, angels.

Things like that happened all over Savannah. It's a diverse city in that the present does not abandon the past. The charm remains southern, and its past continues to fascinate its visitors.

Tap your angels for the max experience of Savannah…and the southeastern U.S. in general.

Alaska

All-you-can-eat crab legs. That's one of my most profound memories of Alaska.

We did a cruise sailing from Seward, Alaska to Victoria, B.C. We love cruising, and this one didn't disappoint.

ANGEL TRIPPIN'

Ariel and Sandalphon made sure that we got quite the show from Mother Nature. We cruised past soaring mountains, massive glaciers, and wildlife in areas that humans can only reach by boat or a drop from a plane. Angels constantly poked us to view so many details of this amazing wilderness.

In addition to the incredible scenery of Alaska, our choice of shore excursions was like picking out Christmas gifts. One that we chose was to go out on a crab boat and learn how they harvest crabs.

Like most people, we'd watched television reality shows highlighting that sometimes dangerous career. Where they took us for the excursion, though, was on much tamer waters.

After learning the ins and outs of crabbing, we settled in at their shoreline restaurant to partake of all-you-could-eat crab. There's no describing the taste of freshly caught crab. We couldn't get enough.

My husband is allergic to shellfish, but he threw caution to the wind on this day and ate crab like he'd never get it again. In the thrill of the feast, I suddenly remembered his allergy.

He was nonplussed...and kept eating.

Arriving back at the ship, my husband started showing signs of his allergy. Thanks to Raphael, though, a trip to the ship's doctor never happened.

If you haven't cruised Alaska, put it on your bucket list. If it isn't impressive enough on its own, the angels can make it truly unforgettable.

CH JODI M DEHN

The Southwest

The U.S. desert southwest casts a wide variety of landscapes and attractions and angel interaction. There's no way that I can cover it all, but I will give you a smattering.

As you know, Elvis made one town famous, along with all the mobsters that helped build the casinos. If any place needs angels, it's Las Vegas - Sin City.

There's so much going on in Las Vegas. There are so many things that can go wrong in Las Vegas. The saying "what happens in Vegas stays in Vegas" was coined for a reason.

You genuinely need protection here. Make sure that you are armed and ready with Michael. I'm sorry if that sounds harsh and a bit unnecessary, but it really isn't. You need a lot of protection in Vegas.

Pickpockets run rampant. Prostitutes hang on every corner, wait in every hotel lobby, and walk the strip day and night. Bartenders, and even the strangers beside you at a bar, place roofies in your drinks. It can happen to anyone - men and women. You really need to be on your guard.

The National Finals Rodeo was in full swing the last time we were there. There were cowboys and cowgirls everywhere.

Getting an Uber was a challenge, especially late afternoon and into the evening. Raphael came through for us in fine form, though.

ANGEL TRIPPIN'

We Ubered to a restaurant located in another large hotel complex. The driver dropped us off at a door about as far away from the restaurant as possible.

After walking several blocks to the complex, our daughter realized she'd left her phone in the Uber. Immediately she was on the phone, and her husband was heading back to the drop-off location. The rest of us proceeded to the restaurant. Surprisingly, the Uber driver found her phone wedged between the seats and was heading back to the drop-off as our daughter connected with him.

There was no doubt angels worked both ends of that situation.

Other times the angels showed up for me as Earth angels. We could be anywhere, and it just took a look from somebody that would tell me that I needed to pay attention - to be present. Whether it was a security person, bouncer, server, bartender, or someone sitting at a slot machine or standing on a street corner. They would let me know if I should be more aware of my surroundings.

I'd also receive looks telling me all was well.

Earth Angels are prevalent in Las Vegas. Make sure that you are on the watch for them. If you feel like you're getting a message from one of them, remember a "thank you" is absolutely necessary. Just give them a slight nod of the head. They'll know. They'll understand your message.

There's a lot that I could say about angels in other parts of the Southwest. I want to focus on one location, though: Red Rocks.

Red Rocks is a natural amphitheater right outside of Denver. It's impressive enough in the daytime. But at night, under the stars attending a concert, it's unbelievable.

Chamuel helps you to experience Red Rocks with the wonder of a child. The sound is perfect. The ambiance is excellent. The entire experience takes you back to the magic and wonder of being a kid.

Thank you, Chamuel.

The East Coast

Say "East Coast" and most people immediately think of New York City.

At the time of this writing, I've been there four times with different groups of people each time, making each trip very interesting. The angels presented themselves in different ways with each group. Yet, depending on the location we were in, there were similarities.

On one trip, when there were four moms and four daughters, we found ourselves at St. Patrick's Cathedral. Just walking in there gave you a feeling of stepping into a celestial space. If that wasn't enough, one of the choirs was rehearsing.

I love men's choirs. Their voices give power to certain music like nothing else. On this day, it was a men's and boy's choir rehearsing an acapella piece. It was the sound of angels. The eight of us sat in one of the pews, mesmerized. At the conclusion of the

ANGEL TRIPPIN'

piece, even the daughters were teary-eyed. Sandalphon brought us to this place to experience a beautiful moment in the city that never sleeps.

We did some shopping on that same trip. It wouldn't be a trip to the Big Apple without shopping.

We wandered into a store that sent the daughters scrambling to find tops and dresses and pants to try on. As the moms waited to see the results, one mom happened to look up. There were mirrors on the ceilings above the dressing rooms. We had the girls out of there in about two minutes. When I asked the sharp-eyed mom what made her look up, she shrugged her shoulders and said, "a little bird told me."

Thank you, angels.

My husband and I went to NYC right after September 11th. I won the trip…a total surprise.

It was a whirlwind trip. We were in and out of NYC in a little over 24 hours. Our flight was paid. There was a limousine waiting at the airport for us. Our hotel was on-the-house. And we had tickets to Sting's Rainforest concert at Carnegie Hall. The only thing we were on the hook for was food.

A visit to Ground Zero was a must. 9/11 impacted me greatly. I am a military veteran. I come from a military veteran family, and 9/11 cut me to the core.

CH JODI M DEHN

Visiting Ground Zero in New York City had a similar impact on me. I knew that it would. I didn't even think to call in my angels as I was already so emotionally and mentally bound up before we got there. Not knowing what I would see or feel, the angels were out of sight, out of mind for me.

Yet they still protected me.

They made sure that mentally and emotionally I was eased into the situation, so that I could deal with it. So it wouldn't traumatize me further.

When you are as in tune with your angels as I am (I work with them 24/7), the angels come to you, with and without you even asking. They know what's in your heart. They know what's in your mind. They know what you need. Thanks to my angels, the 9/11 experience was incredible. Incredibly sad and incredibly humbling, and seriously life-changing.

Boston, on the other hand, proved to be a surprise. My husband and I love history, and Boston is jam-packed with it.

We tend to shy away from downtown areas of big cities, but not Boston. It holds a different excitement from New York City. Where NYC sparkles with its glitz and glam, Boston thrills with the many ethnic neighborhoods all within walking distance.

Here the angels seemed as amazed as us. I was reading excitement in their messages. They were almost giddy. Maybe that made the visit more exciting. Either way, Boston is on our return visit list.

ANGEL TRIPPIN'

As for most of the rest of the East Coast, there's an "attitude" there that makes it what it is. I love the directness and bluntness of the people from this part of the country. They're a far cry from the passive/ aggressive attitudes found in most of the Midwest. If you're not well acquainted with the East Coast vibe, you might be easily offended by it.

I always get Gabriel tuned in to help with those East Coast conversations. Sometimes I've found it necessary to bring in Zadkiel to help translate some of the intentions behind those conversations. I would never walk away from any of those conversations, though. Once you understand the intentions, you'll find yourself in the company of some very wonderful people.

The West Coast

I am a wild west fanatic. I've been traveling the western U.S. since I was a kid.

One year on a trip out west with my husband, we stopped in Bannock, MT. Bannock was once a thriving town. Now it's a ghost town...a real ghost town. Montana designated it as such, and state employees maintain the deserted buildings.

You're free to roam the town. Most of the buildings remain safe enough to go inside.

I'd called in the angels before exploring. I had a feeling that it might be necessary. I found out that message was my angels telling me to bring them in. They do work in mysterious ways sometimes.

CH JODI M DEHN

We got to the saloon and were intrigued by the original bar inside. Jokingly my husband told me to knock. I call it the "shave and haircut - two bits" knock.

I'd thought about knocking on the bar but decided to knock on the wall instead. I'd just finished the first part of the knock when Bam! The "two bits" knock responded from the other side. My husband and I stood there grinning at each other.

We moved on to some of the other buildings. Approaching the Hotel Meade, I could feel a warning.

Unlike most hotels from that era, you have to climb a few steps to enter. We toured the first floor, and it was when we went up to the second floor that the reason for the warning surfaced. I was at the top of the stairs; my husband was coming up behind me. Suddenly, something or someone pushed him, almost knocking him down the stairs. We didn't find any history about Hotel Meade that might explain the identity of the culprit.

Moving farther west and south, there's Virginia City, NV. It was a destination for a paranormal event for us.

My heart soared there.

You feel like you stepped back into the mid to late 1800s. Definitely a thriving wild, wild west environment.

On weekends locals walk the streets dressed in period clothes. They talk to you as if you're in another time.

ANGEL TRIPPIN'

Because we planned to investigate paranormal activity, we did a solo activity visiting the Mackay Mansion. Quite the history with that place. I won't go into it here though.

Johnny Depp booked it for a month's stay. He didn't believe in spirits. Well, he only lasted three nights. He believes in spirits now.

Again, with angels on alert, we took the tour with a remarkably knowledgeable tour guide. We were standing in the drawing room when we suddenly heard footsteps walking above us. We were the only ones in the mansion.

There was a picture of a very stern woman on the mantel shelf next to us. Our tour guide informed us that it was a former maid in charge of the other household staff. The photograph of her was taken after she died, which explained the look on her face.

She became our tour companion. Her presence remained with us until we left the building.

There's more...

The bedrooms were on the second floor. One of the children's rooms was filled with dolls...creepy dolls. It seems like they're always creepy dolls in these older places. We looked around the room from the doorway as we were not allowed to enter the room. Suddenly one of the more intense dolls moved.

Thank you, angels, for keeping us sharp.

There are many more stories from the wild west town of Virginia City and other locales, but I'll save those for another time.

CH JODI M DEHN

The Pacific Northwest

Rainforest territory in the U.S.A. seems like a mistake. If it is, it makes for a wonderland adventure.

Except for the younger age of this area, the weather reminds me so much of Great Britain. Maybe South America, too, but I have yet to venture there.

Consequently, it can be dark. The ambience can be dark.

Gabriel should be called upon for your planning and adventures here. Gabriel lends you his creative side and his penchant for positive experiences.

On one visit we toured Seattle's underground.

For those who don't know, the underground was once the normal street level for Seattle. In that, it takes on many different facets of the city.

Like many cities in this country, it holds a darker past as well as the light of courage and resiliency of the people who survived. Moving through the tour, the emotions trapped there touched me on several occasions. Jophiel stepped up to help me discern what I was receiving. I found it very powerful and moving.

Moving on, places like Pike's Market team with bustling energy. Patrons and vendors are constantly in motion. Quite the opposite of the underground. It's clear that Haniel finds a niche with each vendor.

ANGEL TRIPPIN'

Traveling out into the landscape of the Pacific Northwest, one finds majesty. From the volcanoes to the pounding surf of oceanside, it always gives you an untamed exhilaration. Clearly Ariel moves back and forth between his dark and light side as you experience the natural wonders of the Pacific Northwest.

CHAPTER 14

Exploring with the Angels

Castles

Fascinating places, those castles are. Each one is as unique and different as the people who built them and lived there.

We're talking international castles.

First, you learn a castle's history because you will go through them on tours. Be open and cognizant as you proceed on the tour with your angels present. The angels will give you little cues about why something is important besides what your tour guide tells you, and what to look out for. Listen closely to your tour guide, though. You will make the connection with your celestial message.

You're always given time to walk around on your own. Your angels will be so helpful at illuminating things that will be of interest and importance to you.

So many times when you go on these tours, it almost gets overwhelming. There is so much to see, and there is so much to read and so much to absorb. You don't know where to start and stop. The angels are going to help you with that. They are going to guide you to those pieces, to those rooms, to those items, to those readings that are meaningful to you. Those points of interest provide the kind of information that you'll appreciate without getting overwhelmed.

ANGEL TRIPPIN'

For example, we visited Charleville Castle in Ireland on a dark, foreboding day. The castle felt different from other ones that we'd explored. It felt "off."

We were in the library. Beautiful room. I'm partial to libraries.

A member of the group, a psychic, could feel some of the weirdness as well, although she couldn't pinpoint it. So, she got out her dowsing rods. I've used dowsing rods in the past. They are remarkable objects.

As the psychic questioned the energy or energies present with us, she got the word "piano." Another psychic in our group had just heard the faint sound of a piano playing.

As the questioning progressed, the dowsing rods suddenly pointed to me. The spirit that the psychics were communicating with was upset. They were upset that I was present. When one of the psychics questioned me as to why that might be, Gabriel popped into my ear and said, "Classically trained." I am a classically trained pianist. Once I told the group and the spirit this fact, everything shifted.

Having experienced this, the feeling in the castle changed for me. It was no longer "off."

The angels know when you let them guide. They enjoy every castle that you explore. Some castles might not be that interesting at first encounter, but the angels are taking you there for a reason. They will point out to you, even the littlest of gems, why you're there.

So be a prince or a princess with your angels guiding you.

CH JODI M DEHN

Lock Ups

Prisons and jails - you find them all over the world. There is a difference between the facilities in the U.S. and those that are overseas.

I've visited jails in Ireland, England, Russia, and other locations worldwide. Each one has its own unique brand of imprisonment experience.

The second time my husband and I explored Ireland, we once again found ourselves in Cork—a wonderful Irish community. I wasn't feeling 100%, so I didn't tour the Cork Gaol/Jail with the rest of the group. My husband did.

One member of our group captured the most interesting sight when randomly taking pictures inside the jail. She showed it to my husband, who told her she needed to show it to me.

I was ecstatic when she did.

It was an orb. I don't put a lot of stock in orbs, but this one was different. It had a shape in it. The shape was a halo.

First of all, if there's a shape in an orb, it's an angel orb. Second, if the shape is a halo, it's confirmation of that.

I can't say which Archangel it might have been, since I wasn't there to assess the surroundings, the feelings, and the presence of the moment. My past experiences made me think it was Michael, Raphael, Chamuel, or Jeremiel.

That was a very rare occurrence, but an occurrence nonetheless.

ANGEL TRIPPIN'

Let's go stateside.

As of this writing, Joliet prison in Joliet, IL, is my most current prison visited. Joliet housed inmates for 144 years, built-in 1858 by the inmates. It closed in 2002. The history there is incredibly dark. Some of the most notorious criminals in our nation's history served their time there.

The feeling, even as you're approaching it, feels negative. I believe that prisons and jails are inherently negative just by the nature of the crimes of the inmates. Prisons can be affected, however, by the energy of the community that surrounds the facility.

When prisons were first built, they were always built away from the local towns to protect the residents. As time went on and communities grew, these facilities found themselves absorbed within the communities.

When a community has a more positive light, depending on its development, growth, and outside influences, it may turn dark when it combines with the energies of the correctional facility. The opposite could happen with the facility; if there's significant influence from the surrounding community, it could assume a more positive vibe.

In the case of Joliet, due to the horrific events that happened there, I believe that the area surrounding Joliet Prison was more affected by the prison than vice versa. Parts of the Joliet community are lovely, with beautiful residential areas, thriving residential areas, but the area immediately around the abandoned prison—let's just say you wouldn't want to walk the streets alone at night.

CH JODI M DEHN

Even as you move into Joliet prison, you feel a cloud descend. It's heavy.

You'll find bullet holes and busted windowpanes. Sadly, kids have vandalized a great deal of the prison. There's graffiti everywhere, which adds to the darkness.

When we investigated the first night, I was in a cell in the west cell block. I'd been physically touched, so I was trying to communicate with the inmate responsible. In the middle of the attempted conversation, one of my daughters ran to find me.

"We just heard 'angel,'" she said. "I think they want to talk to you."

Moving quickly to the end of the cell block where the voice had come through to others, I initiated a conversation. Sadly, I was almost immediately interrupted by a "time's up" signal from our lead investigators.

Returning the second night, I attempted once again to make contact. After spending ten minutes trying to facilitate a conversation again, I came up short.

I could tell there was a presence there. I couldn't tell if it was a spirit or an angel. Generally, I can discern which one I'm communicating with, but not in this case.

It was soon time to change locations again, so we moved outside.

ANGEL TRIPPIN'

My daughter, once again, came looking for me. Her husband was in contact with five inmates who wanted to cross over. His energy wasn't sufficient to make it happen on his own. We joined him. Together the three of us were successful in helping these souls to cross.

My daughter and son-in-law connected with the spirits, and I connected with Azrael and Gabriel. When the inmates crossed, my daughter and her husband saw, with their third eye, each of the souls ascending. With my third eye, I saw a brilliant white light like a mushroom cloud explode. I knew that the angels opened the portal to allow the ascension.

Museums

Buildings that house the world's stories and histories contain multi-faceted spiritual energies. These institutions across the globe remind us of the past and give us the details of who, why, when, where, and how people survived or not in other times.

Sandalphon pops up a lot for me in museums. It doesn't matter if the museum is historical or art based. Sandalphon, with his love of music, helps me to connect dots when I explore each room and each piece in each room. It may be because Sandalphon oversees the music of the world. In that, he's viewed as the Middle Man.

Given music is the universal language, it's only appropriate that Sandalphon joins us in our museum explorations.

Gabriel also shows his presence, given his penchant for writers and creativity. His role as chief communicator for understanding provides you with an enlightened experience within these walls.

When we toured the Vatican in all of its vastness, it was quite evident to me when these two archangels took the role of tour guides for me. They navigated me to certain paintings and sculptures, and adornments that I might not have otherwise given a second look. My husband was guided to some similar ones and some different ones. We had a most interesting conversation afterward, comparing notes.

Open yourself to your angels' presence. It makes the cost of admission priceless.

Cemeteries

A lot of people are creeped out by cemeteries. I find them intriguing.

Cemeteries tell stories...stories of people, stories of families, stories of towns, etc. I generally call on Azrael and Zadkiel when researching these final resting places.

A disclaimer here with Azrael: make your intentions very clear and positive. Call him "in light and love." Azrael can turn dark if your intentions don't specify positivity. He is known as the Angel of Death.

What happens when I call Azrael and Zadkiel for guidance develops into a two-realm event. Azrael points out those who possibly still need to cross over. If you're so inclined, with Azrael's help, you can make that happen. And if the spirit is willing, that's where Zadkiel enters. Zadkiel helps you to discern that intention.

You could encounter many angels as you move through these quiet places. I've never been afraid to be in a cemetery. I find them to be places of peace and tranquility.

When I was stationed at Ft. Myer, VA, Arlington National Cemetery was our backyard. The prestigious Army honor guard (The Third Herd to Army folk) reside at Ft. Myer. Often on weekends, my walk would take me through the different sections of Arlington. Angels guided me to particular grave sites from which the soldier, sailor, airman, and marine's story would be given to me. This experience couldn't have been more humbling.

Another cemetery that moved me is in Savannah, GA, called the No Name Cemetery by the locals. It's a big, square-shaped park in the middle of Savannah where slaves were buried in mass graves. The sadness is overwhelming. That day Chamuel accompanied in order for love to surround those graves.

Angels like Azrael and Zadkiel stand ready to help through these profound experiences.

Caves

Caves are as interesting as they are diverse. There are sea caves, glacier caves, lava caves, ice caves, talus caves, and more.

I've been in caves that foster stalactites and stalagmites, crystal caves, and mystery caves.

No matter what type of cave you're exploring, you will get a different vibe from your angels. Generally, Ariel claims the status of Archangel of Nature. Assuming either the male or female role, Ariel is charged with protecting and healing animals and plants. He/she also cares for the natural elements like water and wind. In that capacity, Ariel moves us to care for the environment.

I tend to shy away from Ariel, though, as he/she is also connected to the occult and mysticism. Mysticism is neither here nor there for me. I draw the line at the occult, though.

Having said that, I have called on Ariel several times with a great deal of prefacing of my intentions. I clearly state at least three times in my intentions "in light and love" to bring clarity to my message.

My use of Ariel, particularly with caves and mines, focuses on guiding me to respect the natural wonders. I also request discernment of these natural phenomena to understand their purpose better. Ariel always comes through.

My final word on outdoor sites and Ariel would be to use him/her sparingly and with positive intentions to foster a positive relationship with our environment.

Winter Adventure

I'm including this adventure because of the spiritual vision my husband and I were graced with.

Shortly after we were married, we headed north to go dog sledding with a well-known Arctic explorer. My husband secured the trip through a fundraising silent auction.

ANGEL TRIPPIN'

What a thrill ride!

After receiving our safety briefing the first morning, we headed out to meet the dogs. We were a party of six from all across the country.

Our lead directed me to the sled my husband and I would share. After a brief meeting with the dogs, who were amped up to start running, our lead instructed me in hand signals, brakes, and commands.

Now it was my turn. With the lead still holding the sled and the dogs, I stepped onto the back of the sled. As he let go of the sled, the dogs let go of their restraint and were off.

The lead kept yelling to give the command and hit the brake, which I was frantically doing...to no avail. Given my light weight, the dogs thought they had free rein to go.

The lead popped on his skis, caught up to me, and stopped the dogs. Whew.

Needless to say, my husband drove the team for the rest of the adventure. I walked, ran, or briefly rode as part of the team.

I can't say I wasn't frightened when the dogs took off. I can say that the angels were in control of them and me the entire time, though. Their presence was apparent.

CH JODI M DEHN

On the last day, when we were out sledding, we crossed another frozen lake. I captured a photo of my husband handling the team. The angels graced us with the appearance of a Native American spirit in the crisp winter sky behind my husband. The angels were thanked for a perfect ending to our adventure.

CHAPTER 15

Unpackin' with the Angels

Home, sweet home!

You've had a wonderful trip. Just about everything worked out the way that you hoped. The majority of your expectations were met. You have tons and tons of beautiful memories that you will share with family and friends and carry with you for the rest of your life.

If you haven't already done so, I recommend thanking your angels now. Thank them for all the different little milestones on your trip. Thank them by name, and as you reflect on your experiences, you will know which ones to thank.

Do they need your thanks? No, they're your angels. They help you because they're about light and love and want us to lead the best possible lives. Thanking them is just such a great practice to get into. It helps you realize how thankful and grateful you are for what was planned for you.

Remember, go all the way back to the beginning. They helped you to prep and plan what you experienced along the way. I would love to be an angel sitting on your shoulder to see and hear about your extraordinary adventures.

And, of course, now that you're home, there are some things that you need to do to settle yourself back into your non-travel life.

CH JODI M DEHN

It's always a bit of a letdown when you return home because the excitement is over, and the new friends aren't there anymore. Keep in mind, though, that you met some wonderful people you are now in contact with that you may even share more trips and adventures with, so just take a moment and journal some of that. Whatever your favorite way is to tuck that information away, besides in your mind, is perfect.

Then at the same time as you're journaling—or however you're doing this—note which angels were probably responsible for that little memory, that little tidbit that still has you excited. That way, as the days go on and you long to be back on the trip, you can pull out that journal and relive it in your words. Just sit, close your eyes, and remember it. See it with your third eye. Call in your angels to share in the experience with you again as you move through your adventure.

And finally, one more time, thank your angels.

I could go on with many more places, but it's time for you to get out there. Keep these Angel Trippin' tips with you. Start planning your next trip. This time with the angels. Their bags are always packed!

ANGEL TRIPPIN'

Angel Glossary

Michael

As the leader of the Archangels, Michael is often depicted with a sword. Call upon Michael when you need protection, strength, and clear boundaries to release what no longer serves in your life. Michael helps us to reconnect with our confidence, releasing fears and doubts and illuminating the light from within.

Gabriel

As the Archangel of visions and clarity, call upon Gabriel when you are needed to see a situation more clearly, tap into your intuition, or bring your dreams and ideas into reality. Gabriel is a powerful way to connect to Divine messages and guidance. This Archangel is a messenger of the highest order and can aid you in communicating with clarity and compassion.

Raphael

Known as the healer of the Archangels, Raphael can be called upon in times of sickness, not only of the body but of the heart and spirit as well. Raphael is a healing presence, and also a strong protector of travelers. Ask Raphael to guide you on your path to keep you from harm's way.

Uriel

As the Archangel of wisdom, Uriel comes in with a flaming sword to remove the obstacles holding you back. Uriel helps to transmute feelings of anger, despair, and fear into their positive counterparts to bring about personal transformation. This support brings about positive change in our lives and helps to enhance our inner strength and resilience.

Chamuel

As the Archangel of adoration and courage, Chamuel helps you to practice self-love and self-adoration and embrace peaceful energies when feeling worn thin. Chamuel reminds us to leave room for ourselves in the love we pour into the world. In doing so, Chamuel supports us in releasing old wounds, habits of self-sacrifice and abandonment, and providing courage to overcome obstacles.

Jophiel

As the Archangel of beauty, Jophiel helps us to see the beauty and truth in all things. Sometimes we allow negative thoughts to cloud our minds. When connecting with Jophiel, we can see our thoughts, emotions, and circumstances more clearly. This clarity inspires creativity and appreciation, enhancing our ability to find gratitude for the beauty around us.

Zadkiel

As the Archangel of comfort, prayer, and abundance, Zadkiel helps us to gently release the grip of depression and anxiety in our lives. Zadkiel helps us manifest what we desire in our life, freeing us from the chains of negativity and reminding us to forgive those who have wronged us. This freedom encourages calm and productive communication, even with opposing views at hand.

ANGEL TRIPPIN'

Angel Scents

Michael - Sandalwood, spices, clove, and incense

Gabriel - Super Lavender, True Lavender, banana, sweet orange, Bulgarian rose, black spruce, fish

Raphael - Jasmine, lily of the valley, mint, bergamot, and thyme

Uriel - Cinnamon, black & chili pepper, vanilla, clove, cumin, curry, fig, garlic, maple syrup, nutmeg

Chamuel - Honey, strawberries, and rose

Jophiel - Rosemary, roses, and jasmine

Zadkiel - Violet, pine, incense (sandalwood, myrrh, rosemary blend), coffee, peppermint

Fallen Angels - Sulfur, rotten eggs, blood

For information on other Archangels, go to chaplainjodi.me.

About the Author

Jodi Dehn is an intuitive empath, paranormal investigator, motivational speaker, life coach, published author, ordained pastor and former U.S. Army Chaplain. She had her first angel encounter at age four, which planted the seeds for her decades-long work as an angel lightworker. Her work with angels and her military experiences led to the creation of Survivor Angels.

Jodi's passionate goals for Survivor Angels are to strengthen and support trauma survivors and others who struggle with life's challenges. Through Survivor Angels, Jodi offers loving support to help you escape life's negative energies, and engage positive abilities and gifts that have always been present.

She earned her Master of Divinity degree from Luther Seminary in Saint Paul, MN in 1996. She lives in Minnesota.

Survivor Angels hosts a daily blog (Cerebrations), weekly podcast, and other celestial resources. You can find Jodi's angel work at chaplainjodi.me and Survivor Angels - Chaplain Jodi on Facebook, Instagram, TikTok, Pinterest, YouTube, and wherever you listen to your podcasts.

Read more at https://www.chaplainjodi.me/.

www.ingramcontent.com/pod-product-compliance
Lightning Source LLC
Chambersburg PA
CBHW022119090426
42743CB00008B/916